Phenomenally U:
A Young Woman's Guide to
being Smart, Safe, and
Successful in College.
By Lacey C. Clark!
www.phenomenally-u.com

Table of Contents

INTRODUCTION

phenomenal |fə'nämənəl|

adjective

1 very remarkable; extraordinary

Many young women go to College to find themselves but end up losing themselves. Find your PHENOMENAL! Hi! I'm Lacey C. Clark! Some call me "Sister Lacey!" (yes, the exclamation is part of my name) because I am like a big sister to young women and teen girls today! My company is Sisters' Sanctuary. I am an award-winning speaker, author, and life coach. I am committed to supporting you in making healthier lifestyle choices as you navigate these very important years of your life, the college years. I want you to be safe, smart, and successful. I want you to be #PHENOMENALLYU.

I went to New York University for my undergraduate studies and it was one of the best experiences of my life. I learned so much about myself and others in my college years and I wouldn't trade them for anything in the world. I studied abroad in Paris, I explored NYC, I met a lot of cool people (including one who is still my good friend today), I fell in love, I cried, I laughed, I created films, I joined clubs, I created clubs, I lost weight, I gained weight, I organized trips, I went to a lot of cool events, but most importantly, I grew up. In those four short years, I became a woman. I learned there was a lot of me to love. I even bought my own toilet paper and deodorant for the first time. :) Open yourself up to learn more about who you are.

I want YOU to love YOU... ALL of you and make your mark on the world! Stamp your place in history by being #phenomenallyu. I'm rooting for you!!! Graduate with honors!! BE YOUR BEST! P.U.! P.U.! P. U.! Let's GOOOOOO! Let's GO P.U.! Let's GO! YES!

At some point, I would like to meet you on your campus. I love doing live talks that will help you to be safe, smart, and successful. Let's stay in touch. I'm on Twitter, Facebook and Instagram @LaceyCClark. I believe in you! YES!

Phenomenally yours,

@LaceyCClark

www.phenomenally-u.com

SAFETY

SAFETY

Lesson 1. LEARN HOW TO HAVE SOBER FUN.

Just because you're going off to college, doesn't mean you have to start downing beers and doing tequila shots to have fun. Sure, many of the popular movies today show college students drinking 24/7, but what they don't show are the headaches, heaving and hangovers. Not only will it make you physically feel bad, but drinking too much can make you fall behind on your schoolwork and possibly get you into some dangerous situations.

The Core Institute, the nation's largest database on alcohol & drug use by college students, reports that 31% of students have missed a class due to substance abuse and 22% have failed a test or exam. More frighteningly, approximately 159,000 college freshmen will drop out of school altogether due to alcohol and drug use. Don't be a statistic.

Drinking too much will also lower your defenses and

alter your normal behaviors. Approximately 70% of students in The Core's study reported having unplanned sex (sex they would not have had if they weren't under the influence) and 20% didn't use precautions even though they practice safe sex when sober.

The National Institute on Alcohol Abuse and Alcoholism also reports that thousands of college students still drink and drive or ride with a drunk driver even though approximately 1, 825 students between the ages of 18 and 24 die each year from alcohol-related unintentional injuries, including motor vehicle crashes.

So why not find an alternative?

There are plenty of things to do with your friends that don't involve getting high. Go shopping, take up a sport, go for a hike, go to the movies or treat yourselves to a spa day. Often, young women will start informal clubs in their dorms that get together to watch movies and TV shows they enjoy. Find other people that enjoy the same hobbies as you or take up a new one.

If you're looking for fun at night, go bowling, shoot pool or see a live music or comedy show. Groupons and other similar online deals are a great way to find new activities to try out at a great price.

It's also important to surround yourself with the right people. If you only hang out with people that love to smoke and drink, that's all they're ever going to want to do. Find friends that don't want to drink all the time and be conscious of who you're spending your time with. You can still have fun without having to drink and the best part is, you will actually remember what you did the next day. If you need help, <u>Narcotics Anonymous</u> (NA) or <u>Alcoholics Anonymous</u> (AA) can help you get free from your dependence on these substances.

What things do you like to do for fun that don't include drinking?

www.phenomenally-u.com

Lesson 2. PRACTICE THE SISTER SYSTEM WHEN GOING TO PARTIES.

Parties can be a fun way to meet new people and release after a stressful week of classes. But even though you want to let loose and have fun, don't forget to be smart about your own safety. With usually large crowds, mostly composed of strangers, lots of alcohol and hormones running amuck, it is important to be proactive about your own safety and the safety of your friends at parties.

Always have a "sister" when going to a party. Make sure you arrive and leave with your sister and watch out for one another during the night. You don't have to stay attached at the hip the whole time, but if one of you goes MIA, you know at least one person will notice and start looking for you. And remember, it works both ways. So no matter how much fun you're having or how attracted you are to that cutie from the football team, if you notice your sister has gone missing, it is your responsibility to look for her until you find her. Treat her like you would treat your real sister.

Set up a system that works for you. You can designate a certain time to meet up during the night to "check in" or periodically check in with each other by text message. You can even determine a secret code word that would only be used in case of emergency. It's important to also devise a strategy ahead of time on what to do if one of you becomes incoherent. It's just a reality that sometimes college students are going to drink until they aren't thinking clearly and right about then, it might seem like a good idea to leave with a sexy stranger. You and your sister need to plan ahead for situations like this and figure out how they should be handled. Someone will always need to keep a level head.

It is always good to have someone looking out for you and vice versa.

Who can you ask to be your party sister or sisters?

Lesson 3. BE AWARE. SOMETIMES SEXUAL ASSAULT CAN BE PREVENTED.

Sexual assault is a reality in today's world. According to the U.S. Centers for Disease Control, one in five college women has been raped at some point in her lifetime and in a typical academic year, 3% of college women report surviving a rape or attempted rape. College women and older women alike have to be vigilant to keep themselves safe.

Some steps in sexual assault prevention may seem like common sense but it's easy to forget or let them slide when you're in a hurry or just not thinking. But no matter how busy or distracted you are, you need to ALWAYS be aware of your surroundings. Take a visual scan of the area before walking to your parked car, getting on an elevator or walking down a desolate street. Be fully present, free from headphones and cell phone talking. Allow your senses to be alert. Check the backseat and underneath your car before getting in. Always carry your cell phone and a protective device like a whistle, mace or stun gun.

Most importantly, trust your instincts. Women have been gifted with a strong sense of intuition, yet often they are afraid or embarrassed to follow their gut. They don't want to seem "crazy" or like they are overreacting when they get a bad feeling about a stranger close to them. If your gut is giving you an uneasy feeling, trust it and get away from the situation as quickly and safely as you can. It is better to be safe than sorry.

I'm asking you to be aware and but not fearful. Fear is no fun and can promote stress but awareness can save your life.

It's also important to remember that not all rapes are perpetrated by complete strangers. In fact, the majority are not. Date rapes and rapes that occur at parties are prevalent in college. Again, this not about living in fear, this information should motivate you to be aware and take control of your own safety.

Whenever going out on a date, make sure someone else knows where you are going and when you should be home. Download an app for your phone like Circle of 6 that allows you to send a "911" message quickly when you get in a dangerous situation or have a friend call you at a certain time to check in. Never go to an isolated place with someone you don't know very well and always have a sister when you go to a party. Keep an eye on one another during the night and make sure you leave together.

And when you are out at a party or club, be sure to never take your eyes off of your drink. Watch the bartender make it and keep it with you at all times. A recent report by the U.S. Department of Justice named drugged encounters as the leading cause of lack of self defense in a sexual assault. College aged women are also named a high risk group because of lack of attention and aggressive stalking by perpetrators at clubs, bars and parties. Don't let yourself or your friend become a statistic. DO NOT leave your drinks unattended.

Your safety is your responsibility and your right. Don't be afraid to protect yourself.

What changes can you make in your life to help prevent the possibility of sexual assault?

SMARTS

SMARTS

Lesson 1. STUDY SMART.

It doesn't matter if you were a straight-A student in high school or if you barely graduated by the skin of your teeth, college is a chance to be a new you, #PHENOMENALLYU, in every way. And that includes your study habits.

If you thought your homework in high school was hard, college work will make it look like a walk in the park. You'll most likely have 4 or 5 classes to keep up with at once and no one is going to be around to monitor you. It will be entirely up to you to make sure you keep up and not fall behind. The best way to do that is too stay organized and study smart.

Every class you enroll in will have a syllabus that lays out the course requirements, grading criteria and schedule. This should become your best friend! Read it through thoroughly at the beginning of the course and keep it handy so you can refer to it often. Mark important dates like quizzes, tests and project due dates on your calendar.

Keep all of your class materials organized in binders with sections for notes, handouts, quizzes and projects. Highlight pertinent parts of your textbooks and mark important pages with tabs for easy reviewing later. Take detailed written notes in class or use a voice recorder to capture the professor's lecture so you can listen to it again and again.

Or if you're more electronically-inclined, use a laptop or one of the many note taking apps available on your Ipad such as iA Writer, Evernote and Simplenote to type your notes quickly during class. Many of these apps even allow you to take photographs or draw diagrams with your hands or a stylus. Be sure to save all of your notes in separate folders for each class and always a run a backup onto an external hard drive to protect against computer crashes.

Most importantly, stay ahead of the game. If you know

you have a test coming up on Friday, don't wait until 10:00 at night on Thursday to start studying. Make a study schedule ahead of time and allow a little time each day to study one or two sections of material. Make flash cards or use a flashcard app on your phone to review important terms and definitions. Find a group or partner that you can study with. Campus tutors are also available to help you. Also, your professor has office hours. Use them to build a relationship and to connect to your course material.

Take ownership of your education and be motivated to do a good job. Your success is totally in your hands. Failing a class is a waste of money and resources. You will not get your money back. Excel. GET THAT A! Set the G.P.A and make it happen! YES!

Are you a smart studier? What are some ways you can improve your study habits?

Lesson 2. BE STRATEGIC ABOUT WHAT CLUBS, SORORITIES AND INTERNSHIPS YOU JOIN.

College is a great time to explore new hobbies and develop old ones. With a literal plethora of clubs, sports teams, sororities and organizations to join, there is something for everyone. But before you run off and start signing up left and right, take some time to consider what is going to benefit you in the path you want to pursue and what is going to look good to potential employers down the road.

After graduation, you will be searching for your "dream job" and employers will be looking at your college records to decide whether or not they want to hire you. Not only will your grades matter, but also what activities did you participate in, what positions did you hold and what honors were you awarded? If you want to pursue business, employers might like to see leadership or public speaking clubs on your resume. Or if you want to pursue veterinary medicine, volunteering at a shelter or taking an internship at a veterinary clinic could make you stand out from the crowd.

Even choosing which sorority you rush can be an important decision. Choose one that is respected, with a strong history and a good alumni network. They could potentially lead to important connections when you are ready to look for a job.

College is about having fun so choose activities that you will enjoy but don't forget to also choose ones that will help you succeed in your future plans.

What clubs and organizations can you join that will help you achieve your goals?

Lesson 3. LOOK FOR MENTORS IN AND AROUND CAMPUS TO KEEP YOU FOCUSED AND SUPPORTED WITH YOUR GOALS.

A mentor is someone who you trust to counsel and guide you in your life. They can help you with your career, your relationships, your religion or just life in general. Typically, a mentor is older than you and further ahead on the path that you desire to take in your life. Mentors are usually someone you look up to, but they go beyond just being a role model. In addition to living a life that is a model for your own, mentors become actively involved with you, giving advice and offering opportunities to learn whenever possible.

It is important to look for mentors when you get to campus because they can help you navigate through the chaos and confusion that can be college life. Mentors can be anyone from a college professor to a local business owner so be sure to keep your eyes open wide and be open to finding a mentor anywhere.

The most important thing to look for when choosing a mentor is commonality. You will want someone guiding you that is where you want to be and has been where you are. Find someone who is in the career or job field you are interested in and find out how they got there. Ask them if they'd be willing to meet with you periodically to give advice and be available for help when you have questions.

And don't count out students. Sometimes the best mentors can be an older student, a senior or graduate student, who is still fairly close to you in age but has been through more experiences with school and life. A mentor's job is to help keep you focused on your goals and to support you as you work toward them so make sure you choose someone who is encouraging but will keep you on your toes. You don't need someone who will just be your friend; you need someone who will push you to succeed!

Where are some places you can look for a mentor at your school?

SELF-RESPECT

SELF-RESPECT

Lesson 1. CELEBRATE SELF CARE.

It is absolutely imperative to always remember to carve out time for yourself, to treat YOU like a queen. Take the opportunity to focus on enjoying what you like and love. Taking the time to practice self-care allows you to replenish your energy mentally and physically and helps you approach any situation with balance and peace.

Figure out what things make you happy and set aside specific time to indulge in those activities. Take a long candlelit shower with your favorite body wash, go for a nature walk, get a massage, read a book you enjoy, the options are endless. The most important part is that it is relaxing and pampering to YOU.

Often when we get stressed and overwhelmed, we often stop doing basic things for ourselves like getting enough sleep and eating right. Ironically, these are the times when we need to be doing these things the most!

No matter how busy you get or how worried you are over something, make sure you don't slack on the important things. Eat healthy meals regularly, get a good night's sleep and take care of your body and mind. While over nighters can be fun, they are not healthy in the long run. Ignoring any of these things will only make you feel more worn down and unable to handle stress properly.

Take care of you like you would a cherished friend. Allow yourself to rest, breath and relax when you need to and make time to foster your talents and practice the hobbies that you enjoy. Love yourself just as you are. Celebrate Self-love Day! Self-love Day is the 13th of every month. It's a day to anchor into caring for you and only you. It's a day to unplug (that's right, put that phone down for awhile...no texting or tweeting or looking at Facebook), relax, be still and enjoy. You are your number one priority. Make special plans just for you.

Where can you rearrange your schedule and find an hour a day to practice loving and being with YOU? #PHENOMENALLYU!

Lesson 2. LEARN TO SAY "NO", WITH LOVE.

As women, we often feel obligated to say "yes" when we actually want to say "no." We overextend ourselves, trying to please everyone all of the time. Whether it's because we want to be everything to everyone or we're afraid people won't like us if we say no, it is important to learn the power of saying "no" with love.

When we know how to set clear boundaries for ourselves, we are able to let people know what will and will not be allowed. Communicating your boundaries helps others understand that you are someone worthy of respect. It reminds people that you have your own life with your own problems and issues to deal with and that you're not always available 24/7 to help them with theirs. Boundaries are borders. Have you ever felt that a friend or family member had no concept of borders in your relationship? Maybe they think it's okay to ask you to babysit on a Friday night when they know you work a job early on Saturday mornings. Or maybe they continue to borrow money from you over and over again but display no intention of ever paying you back. In these types of situations, saying no is actually the loving thing to do. Constantly giving in to others' whims and taking care of them all of the time prevents them from learning to problem solve and be self-sufficient because they become dependent on you. By saying no, you are helping them to grow and mature as individual people.

Sometimes we need to say, "no" to others to say, "yes" to ourselves. Boundaries are about honoring your integrity and maintaining your peace of mind and emotional well-being. We cannot be any use to anyone else much less ourselves if we are exhausted from overextending ourselves. Agreeing to do things that you don't genuinely want to do undermines your own self-respect and starts a destructive pattern of not listening to your own needs and desires.

Where can you learn to say no in your life?

Lesson 3. CELEBRATE AND HONOR YOUR VALUES.

What's important to you? Values are traits or qualities that are considered worthwhile to you. They represent your highest priorities and deeply held driving forces. In other words, they are your motivation and what is important to you. They can be based on moral beliefs, religion and social norms. At their very basic level, values determine what is considered "right" and "wrong" in your life. They affect your attitude and eventually your behaviors.

If you haven't taken the time to stop and assess your values, now is the time to do so. It's important to move into the next phase of your life at college with a strong sense of who you are and what you value because you will be introduced to a world of new people from different backgrounds. You can always change your values as you learn and gain more life experiences, but it is good to have a solid foundation.

Do you value spending time with your family and friends

or making money and learning new skills? This determination could be important when it comes to accepting a job. Most importantly, knowing your values is crucial when starting a new romantic relationship. If you value fidelity, honesty and respect, you will want to be sure you are dating someone who values the same or else you'll be in for a rude awakening.

Knowing your values helps you communicate well with others, especially with those you love. By knowing what is important to you, you are able to share those with potential friends, partners and employers as a way of establishing what you want and what you expect out of your relationship.

You have the right to celebrate your values. Don't conform to others' beliefs or feel pressured to do things that go against what you stand for. At the same time, allow yourself to explore a new path if you feel deeply called to do so. For example, if you come from a certain religious background and you want to experience something else, try it to see if the shoe fits. College is about learning more of who YOU are and what makes you #PHENOMENALLYU.

Not sure what your values are? Think about the times in your life when you felt the happiest or most proud. Or when you have felt the most fulfilled and satisfied with your life. What specifically about those experiences made them so joyful and memorable? This will give you a glimpse into what you value most.

What values are important to you?

Lesson 4. SISTERHOOD - TREAT EVERY WOMAN LIKE YOU WANT TO BE TREATED.

See other young women in your life as allies and not enemies. If you looked at the next woman as yourself, how would you treat her differently? If you focused on collaboration instead of competition, how would your interactions with other women change?

Have you ever counted the number of times the word, "bitch" is used to demean and belittle another woman on popular reality TV shows? What kind of power does that word have? What do you think the characters really mean when they use that word? If you ever used this word, what do you mean by it? Why is there so much venom and contempt in a room full of women?

Could it be that you disapprove of yourself but instead of admitting that, you find it easier to detest the next woman? If yes, here are three ways to begin to learn how to be accountable to your BODACIOUSNESS and DIVINITY and embrace the same in others:

1.Compare yourself to no one.

Everyone has their own light to shine. Own yours. Focus on creating beauty in your life. You have the power to grow and cultivate delightful moments and experiences in your reality.

How can you create something awesome for yourself today?

2. Don't hate, Celebrate!

Celebrate and honor thyself. When you take the time to lift up your goodness and strengths, you will have no time to hate on and belittle others. Focus on creating your lane and drive well in it!

In what ways can you celebrate your uniqueness this week?

3. See "Her" as You.

Cultivate authentic and supportive relationships with other women. Look for women to admire, support and encourage. Be unapologetic about honoring the greatness and beauty of others without losing yourself.

Who would you like to begin building a better relationship with? What ways can you offer positivity and goodness to the women around you?

SUCCESS

SUCCESS

Lesson 1. INVEST IN YOU.

What do you spend your money on? Clothes and shoes? Books and music? Maybe massages and manicures? Hair and handbags? Do these purchases elevate the quality of your life in any way? Your past purchases will show you what you value. Look at your receipts and notice where you have been spending the bulk of your money. Take a moment to consider it.

You are your best asset. Love yourself enough to gift yourself with purchases that build up your spirit. Figure out what things make you happy and treat yourself every once in awhile. You are worthy of books, music, movies, people, classes, workshops and seminars that enhance you and allow you to be #PHENOMENALLYU.

Do you enjoy the arts? Find some studios in your area that offer drawing classes or schedule a painting party and invite your friends. Love to work out? Invest in some quality running shoes or a treadmill, sign up for Zumba classes or register for a 5k.

Money that is spent on fostering your interests is money well spent. Especially if they will help you develop your talents into a successful career. You may look back and regret buying that neon yellow tank dress but you most likely won't regret taking that public speaking course.

Just as you wouldn't mind investing money in a house because it will develop value over time, so will you. Every enhancement you make to yourself is an investment in your future. Don't be afraid to put the time and money in now because it will pay off in multitudes later.

In what ways can you invest in your greatness today?

Lesson 2. WORDS HAVE POWER.

Words have the power to hurt or heal. This includes the words that come to mind when you think about yourself. Have you ever stopped to take inventory of the thoughts that go through your mind when you look in the mirror, at a photo of yourself or are talking about yourself to others? If you are speaking negatively about yourself (even if it is just in your head), how do you expect others to treat you positively? So many of us have a negative tape playing over and over in our minds subconsciously that we hardly even notice it.

But what you really think and feel will eventually seep out when you speak whether you are conscious of it or not. Purposely embracing new and positive vocabulary will begin to help shift your thoughts to new possibilities. It can begin healing the brokenness and negative self-talk.

Next time a negative thought goes through your mind, consciously stop it and replace it with a more positive thought. It may seem false or fake to you at first, but the more you practice it, the more natural it will become. And eventually all the negative thoughts will fade away quietly.

Do you want to bring others down? Or do you want to be a ray of light, inspiring people to be the best they can be?

Role Models create possibilities. Make sure you are promoting positive possibilities with your words.

Here are a few power phrases to get you started:

I am POWERFUL!
I create my own reality.
I attract good people and great experiences.
I love ME.
I am Beautiful.

What words can you use on daily basis to bring love, goodness and beauty to yourself and others?

Lesson 3. INTEGRITY. INTEGRITY. INTEGRITY.

integrity |in'tegritē| noun 1 the quality of being honest and having strong moral principles; moral uprightness.

Who are you when no one is watching? Do you behave differently around others than you do on your own? If you watched a movie of your life, what kind of character would you be? Would you love or hate her?

Being of quality character is important when being a role model for others, as well as to have success in your own life. It does not mean you have to be perfect or that you can't be human. We are all beautifully human. We don't get everything "right." But, do your words align with your actions and do you try your best to be your best? Are your actions and behaviors in line with your values in life?

If you walk around telling everyone that you value honesty but you lie every chance you get, you are not being authentic. In order to be the very best version of ourselves that you can be, it is important to be consistent in your beliefs and behaviors. You never know who could be watching. If your 10-year-old sister sees you busting your behind to get good grades and earn a scholarship, she may just do the same thing because you've set a good example. And even if no one else is watching, you still have to look at yourself in the mirror every day.

Be intentional about your character. Decide what values make up "good character" to you and live your life in a way that demonstrates those values. Be consistent in who you are and don't change your values based on a person or situation. Think of the people you enjoy being around and why that is. Be the kind of person that you would want to meet and have in your life.

In what ways can you begin identifying your values and living and behaving in alignment with them?

SEX

SEX

Lesson 1. SEX DOES NOT EQUAL LOVE.

If ever there was an area that men and women could differ greatly in, it would be the love/sex debate. Many men can have sex simply for the physical enjoyment it brings while many women find themselves quickly becoming emotionally attached to their sexual partners. Of course this is not an absolute rule and there are plenty of women that can separate sex and feelings, while some men find they cannot.

But any way around it, it is important to remember that sex and love ARE indeed two very separate things. Anyone can have sex without necessarily being in love and people who choose to be celibate until marriage can easily be in love without having sex. So why do the two get confused so often? Hormones. Those lovely chemicals running rampant through our bodies at all times.

The same hormones that get you all hot and bothered can also unfortunately make your heart go pitter pat and cause you to start picturing babies with your sexual partner. This is okay if you plan on continuing to date this person and possibly one day marry them and start a family. But it is important to remember that sex does not automatically mean love. Don't be afraid to discuss your feelings openly with your partner. Share with one another what your expectations are and set some ground rules that are comfortable with both of you. Make sure that both of you are on the same page and that no one is under any delusions of what is actually going on in the relationship.

And never, ever lower your standards or change your beliefs just to satisfy a partner to appear "cool" in their eyes. Often women will try to pretend they are perfectly fine with a "friends with benefits" situation, while in fact they believe they are just biding their time until the guy comes to his senses and realizes he's in love with her. It's a dangerous game of Russian roulette and you don't want to be on the receiving end of that trigger.

The man that truly deserves you will love you because you are YOU, #PHENOMENALLYU, not because you dress in a provocative way or because you are willing to do certain things with him.

How can you make sure you don't confuse sex with love?

Lesson 2. ALWAYS PROMOTE CONDOMS.

It seems like a given in today's society, but believe it or not, condoms can still be a topic of embarrassment for many young women. It is up to us women to protect ourselves from STD's and unwanted pregnancy and there is no shame in that.

Whether you are in a committed relationship or just having a casual fling, asking for a condom is not a hassle, it is your right. After all, if you are responsible enough to be having sex in the first place, then you should be responsible enough to do it safely.

Typically men are the ones that are expected to carry the condoms in their wallet, always "ready" at any time. But there is no law that says a woman can't do the same. Sure, there are some people that would stereotype that as a woman being trashy or "easy," but that's exactly what that is. A stereotype. Not reality.

In reality, a woman who is prepared with condoms (whether they're in her purse or her nightstand), is a responsible woman who cares about herself and her partner. Don't rely on the man to do the right thing and don't fall for any lines about it "not feeling as good" when he wears one. If he is a mature individual, he won't fight you on it and if he's not, you don't need to be with him in the first place.

According to insidehighered.com, a daily publication focused on college and university topics, pregnancies greatly increase the risk of women dropping out of college. In fact, 61% of women who have children while enrolled in college fail to finish their degree because of struggles with finances, time management and emotional stress.

Birth control such as the pill, diaphragms or IUDs can help prevent unwanted pregnancy but the only protection you have against STD's besides celibacy, is using a condom. Don't ever assume that a guy is "clean" just from his appearance. You don't know who he's been with before you and whether or not he used protection. And since most couples don't discuss getting STD tests before having sex (although that would be great!), your best protection is a condom.

Don't let the heat of the moment let you forget the severity of the potential consequences. No moment of pleasure is worth an unplanned pregnancy or a life-threatening health issue.

You want to have sex? Use a condom. Every time. Period.

Lesson 3. DON'T FALL FOR MR. SMOOTHSWEETSLICK.

We've all seen him before. The guy at the party that thinks he is God's gift to women. He's full of line after line and acts like you should be thanking the heavens above that he's even talking to you. But don't think Mr. SmoothSweetSlick is so easy to spot.

Sometimes the more dangerous players are the ones you don't see coming. It's the guy who seems to say and do all the right things. He volunteers for the homeless, he appreciates brains more than beauty (although you truly ARE the most beautiful woman he's ever seen), he wants to wait to have sex.

Sure, it is entirely possible that there are men out there that do mean these things. But there are also a whole lot of men that prey on young college women who they believe to be naive and "easy targets." Especially freshmen.

Be sure you put some time in and do some research

before you go believing everything he says. Do his actions match up with what he's telling you? Does he really seem interested in YOU as a person - your hobbies, your studies, your likes & dislikes? Is he respectful of your physical boundaries? Is he polite to others and seem genuinely interested in helping them?

If a guy is faking it for the sake of "getting some," it won't take long for his true colors to show. Like my mom always says to me, "Time will tell." He will get impatient or bored or both and he will want to move on to another target. Likewise, if a guy is being genuine, he won't mind you being cautious and will most likely respect you even more for it in the long run.

Expect the best from people AND be smart, trust your instincts and take your time to get to know people for who they really are.

What are some traits you can keep an eye on when trying to avoid Mr. SmoothSweetSlick?

Lesson 4. EXPLORING WHO YOU ARE AS A SEXUAL BEING IS HEALTHY AND NATURAL.

College is the time where you learn to face yourself without being under the influence of your parents or guardians. It is your time to really ask yourself, "Who am I?" Self-discovery comes in so many ways. Through laughter, pain, sadness, frustration, joy and pleasure. Many young women give birth to the many layers of their sexuality in college. When you are ready to open that door to that part of who you are, remember that you deserve respect and healthy forms of pleasure. Nothing about you or your bodily functions is dirty, ugly or unnatural. NOTHING!

Young women should be compelled to:
- know how to communicate what you want
- enjoy the sexual experience
- explore, learn and know your body and what makes you tick
- have orgasms
- love your whole body
- feel safe

- know that sex is the most creative force in the world and was divinely designed
- practice the art of receiving and being pleasured

You are NOT an object for someone else's pleasure. You are sacred and need to be respected as such. You are #PHENOMENALLYU.

Sometimes young women explore bisexuality, homosexuality or other non-traditional forms of sexuality. In fact, a recent survey from the Center for Disease Control's National Center for Health Statistics, reported that 14% of women in their late teens and 20's had at least one sexual encounter with another woman. Whatever your experience, be sure to be safe. Your school's women's center or health center can offer you confidential support if needed. Remember, sometimes we learn who we are and who we are not by trial and error. It's okay to define yourself for YOU or not define yourself at all. Experiences are part of self-discovery. Better to tell the truth to yourself now than to lie later.

In what ways can you prepare to be safe as you learn

more about you?

SOCIAL MEDIA

SOCIAL MEDIA

Lesson 1. SOCIAL MEDIA HAS MADE EMBARRASSING EXPERIENCES OF YOUNG WOMEN WORLDWIDE. BE AWARE OF WHAT CAN HAPPEN TO YOU.

Today's world of instant communication and social networking introduces a whole new set of concerns for young women. One of these main concerns is a lack of privacy. These days anyone can find themselves tagged in a photo on Facebook or Twitter where literally the whole world can see. And just because you're not taking the picture, doesn't mean you are safe. Other people at a party can take photos of you without you even knowing it and post them to the internet in a matter of minutes. So much for "what happens at the club, stays at the club."

To keep from finding yourself in an uncomfortable online predicament, make sure you're always aware of your surroundings when you're out. Pay attention to those you're with and those that are around you. You never know when a camera could be pointed right at you. Don't let yourself get out of control by drinking too much. Most embarrassing online photos are of people acting outside their normal character and behaving in a way they most likely wouldn't when sober. So the surest way to prevent being caught in a bad photo is to stay sober enough to be aware of what's going on. Simply put, don't do anything that you wouldn't mind the whole world seeing you do!

What will you do differently the next time you're out to make sure you don't end up in an embarrassing situation online?

Lesson 2. PRIVACY! THE WORLD READS SOCIAL MEDIA... POTENTIAL EMPLOYERS, EXES, FAMILY. BE MINDFUL OF WHAT YOU POST.

Social media is fun. It's an awesome way to share pictures and update friends and family on what's going on in your life. But in today's world of incessant communication, it's very easy to overshare.

It's easy to forget when typing a few words from behind your computer screen or cell phone that the world can see what you are posting. Even social networks with "friends" and "followers" are still open to the public to a certain degree. Many employers these days check out a potential employee's Facebook wall before deciding whether or not to hire them. And what's the first thing you do when you meet someone new that you're interested in? Check them out online.

You may post an embarrassing photo or a negative rant in the spur of the moment and completely forget about it a few days later. But unfortunately, that post is still very much there and very accessible to everyone in (and outside of) your life.

Would you be okay with your new boyfriend's mom seeing your Facebook wall? Would your potential new boss approve of all your tweets?

Besides possibly embarrassing you, oversharing on social media can put you in a dangerous situation. In 2012, WHOA (Working to Halt Online Abuse) reported 394 cases of cyberstalking, with 36% of the victims between the ages of 18 and 31 and a whopping 80% of victims being female. A scary 83% of the cases escalated into other forms of harassment.

It's important to always be mindful of what you are posting on social media and remember everyone who could possibly be reading and seeing it. If it's not something you are 100% comfortable with literally everyone seeing or reading, you most likely shouldn't be posting it.

How can you be more responsible with your social media postings? What can you do differently when posting in social media to protect your privacy?

Lesson 3. USE APPS TO MAKE YOUR LIFE EASIER.

In today's high-tech world, there's an "app" for everything! And for women going off to college, there are five apps that are a must have. Check them out:

Share Your Board – Tired of trying to frantically keep up with your note-taking while your professor is talking? With Share Your Board, you can relax and sit back. Simply snap a picture of any whiteboard with your phone's camera and this app will automatically adjust the screen so you can read it perfectly later while studying.

Quizlet – Studying has gotten a whole lot easier and a whole lot more fun with Quizlet. You just put in the information you need to know and Quizlet will make a set of flashcards that you can review anytime on your phone. The app also includes several games, a progress tracker and sample tests.

Amazon Student – Time to buy your textbooks or ready

to sell your old ones? Amazon Student makes both tasks easier by showing you the best purchase price or trade-in price by simply scanning the book's barcode with your phone's camera. Students also get free two-day shipping for six months on all their Amazon purchases.

Stress Tracker - Stress is a given for all college students but you don't have to let it get the best of you. Stress Tracker will help you track your moods and your most common sources of stress and can display trends in daily, weekly and monthly charts. The app also offers helpful tips and strategies for coping with stress, including a quick six point checklist for those who need relief immediately. All your information is automatically backed up online too so you never have to stress out about losing it.

Circle of 6 – This app is a must have for all women. Once the app is installed on your phone, two simple taps will send out a predetermined text message to 6 contacts of your choice with a call for help getting home and automatically includes an address and map of your exact location. It can also send a request for a phone call to interrupt a bad situation. The app includes pre-programmed national hotline numbers and a local number you can customize for campus security, police or 911.

Lesson 4 USE SOCIAL MEDIA TO YOUR ADVANTAGE

Often, we use social media to express ourselves and engage in superficial conversations, but we can also use social media to help with homework, find out what is going on around campus and to share our accomplishments with family and friends. "Friend" or "follow" your campus clubs and groups. "Friend"or "follow" your school to keep up with school news. Join or create an online group for your studies or major. Keep up with industry trends. Follow people on Twitter who are inspirational to you and are already doing what you want to do. Participate in Tweetchats (conversations on Twitter that are assigned a time and hashtag) that are relevant to you. Social media is a tool that you can use to get the best information to navigate your life with hope, inspiration and ease. Don't waste the opportunity to plug into something GREAT!

How can you begin to use social media to your advantage?

CONCLUSION

So here's to you being #PHENOMENALLYU. These lessons could save your life or at least make it more peaceful, safe and enjoyable.

Your college years can be one of the best and most exciting times of your life. So go ahead, enjoy! Be fierce, be #PHENOMENALLYU, and most of all, remember these lessons:

Safety

- *Learn to have sober fun.* Find something to enjoy that doesn't involve alcohol!
- *Practice the sister system at parties.* Keep an eye out for each other!
- *Be aware.* You may be able to prevent rape and sexual assault.

Smarts

- *Study smart.* Be proactive about your education and strive to do your very best!
- *Be strategic about joining clubs.* Remember to always keep your future in mind!
- *Look for mentors.* Don't be afraid to ask someone who inspires you to support and guide you!

Self-Respect

- *Celebrate self care.* Make sure you take time to love and pamper yourself!
- *Learn to say no with love.*
- *Celebrate and honor your values.* Figure out what is truly important to you and nurture those things in your life!
- *Honor the sisterhood.* See "she" as you.

Success

- *Invest in you.* Spend your money wisely on things that will benefit your future!

- *Words have power.* Be mindful about only speaking good and positive words into your own life and the lives of others!
- *Have integrity.* Be the kind of person that you can be proud of and that you would want to be around yourself. And do it consistently!

Sex

- *Sex does not equal love.* Enjoy yourself! But be smart and be upfront with yourself and your partner about your feelings.
- *Always promote condoms.* Safe sex means no unwanted pregnancies and no STD scares. Period!
- *Don't get caught up with Mr. SmoothSweetSlick.* Entertain men that truly care about and value you as you are.
- *Exploring your sexuality is healthy and natural.*

Discovering who you are as a sexual being is a beautiful process.

Social Media

- *Be aware of what can happen to you on social media.* Keep an eye out around you at all times and make sure you don't end up in a photo you don't approve of!
- *Be mindful of what you post on social media.*
- *Use apps that will make your life easier.*
- *Use social media to your advantage.*

I'd love to hear how these lessons have helped you create a great freshman and sophomore year! <u>Let's stay connected.</u> I'd love to speak on your campus to help you create your own PHENOMENAL Reality! YES!!!! I'm rooting for you! You CAN DO IT!

Let's be friends! @LaceyCClark

#PhenomenallyU "Cr8 Ur Own Reality!"

YES!

NOTES/DREAMS/GOALS

NOTES/DREAMS/GOALS

NOTES/DREAMS/GOALS

NOTES/DREAMS/GOALS

NOTES/DREAMS/GOALS

NOTES/DREAMS/GOALS

NOTES/DREAMS/GOALS

NOTES/DREAMS/GOALS

NOTES/DREAMS/GOALS

NOTES/DREAMS/GOALS

NOTES/DREAMS/GOALS

NOTES/DREAMS/GOALS

NOTES/DREAMS/GOALS

NOTES/DREAMS/GOALS

NOTES/DREAMS/GOALS

NOTES/DREAMS/GOALS

NOTES/DREAMS/GOALS

NOTES/DREAMS/GOALS

NOTES/DREAMS/GOALS

NOTES/DREAMS/GOALS

NOTES/DREAMS/GOALS

NOTES/DREAMS/GOALS

NOTES/DREAMS/GOALS

NOTES/DREAMS/GOALS

NOTES/DREAMS/GOALS

NOTES/DREAMS/GOALS

NOTES/DREAMS/GOALS

NOTES/DREAMS/GOALS

NOTES/DREAMS/GOALS

NOTES/DREAMS/GOALS

NOTES/DREAMS/GOALS

With mantra's like "Because I am sacred," "Celebrate HER Now!" and "Cr8 Ur Own Reality," Lacey C. Clark! is an award-winning speaker, author, life coach and expert in solving the communication challenges between younger and older generations of women of color.

The CEO and Visionary behind Sisters' SanctuaryTM, a holistic empowerment company for women and teen girls inspired by the harmful effects of negative media. Her insights heal wounds and most importantly bridges the gap created by our changing culture. She has shared stages and platforms with, Jill Scott, Hill Harper. Dr. Sonia Sanchez, Les Brown and Dr. Robin Smith of the Oprah Winfrey Show. Lacey! has over twenty years of experience in empowering youth and adults.

Upon graduating from the prestigious New York University, Lacey! received her B.F.A. in film and television. An NYU Founder's Scholar and a recipient of the William H. Cosby Future Filmmakers Award, Lacey's professional career includes working in the Development Department of Spike Lee's 40 Acres and a Mule and teaching overseas in Ghana, West Africa at the National Film and Television Institute.

With over 300 successful keynotes and presentations delivered since 2002, Lacey C. Clark!'s, message of self-love has reached millions of women, young and old. She was even invited to present her company Sisters' Sanctuary at the World Federation of Mental Health Biennial Conference in Melbourne, Australia in February 2003.

In addition to her many accomplishments, Lacey C. Clark! has created various signature events such as the The Phenomenally U Summit for Mothers and Teen Daughters and Fathers and Teen Daughters, The Sisters' Sanctuary Inner BeauTea Party, The Worldwide Self-Love Holiday (I3th Day of every month). The Annual Community Celebration- The I3 Days of Self-love (February I-I3), and The Sisters' Sanctuary Summer Self-love Celebration. She has authored the workbook/journal, *Celebrate HER Now!, An Interactive Guide to Loving Ourselves and Embracing Female Youth of the Hip-Hop Generation*, The Sisters' Sanctuary Self-love 101 Curriculum, The 5 disc collection, *Healing the Gap, Phenomenally U: A Young Woman's Guide to being Smart, Safe, and Successful in College* and the forthcoming Documentary, *"...And in Search of My Phenomenal."*

Sisters' SanctuaryTM has also partnered with Jill Scott's Blues Babe Foundation. Lacey! has also consulted with such agencies as The United Way, The Philadelphia School District, Job Corps, Delta Sigma Theta Sorority, Inc., Temple University, Keystone Mercy Health Plan and The American Cancer Society just to name a few. Her message of empowerment has been shared and viewed in Heart and Soul Magazine, The New York Amsterdam News, The Philadelphia Inquirer and even on BET. She has also gained recognition on Radio One and Clear Channel Radio. Lacey C. Clark! has won numerous awards and has been celebrated by local and state politicians from Philadelphia all the way to California, for her powerful leadership abilities. In the winter of 2007, Clear Channel Radio recognized her as an Unsung Shero.

Currently, she is a contributing writer to such publications such as

The Philadelphia Weekly, AFroElle Magazine, a national columnist at Rolling Out and a Young Women's Empowerment Lifestyle Correspondent for WURD900 AM. Her hobbies include people watching, spa experiences, world travel and dancing to inspirational house music. She resides in Philadelphia, PA.

Are you Emotionally, Mentally, and Spiritually, Ready for College? Get Ready!

Join the Phenomenally U. Membership Program!
Phenomenally U(niversity): Online Life Courses for Pre-college and College Girls Transitioning to Phenomenal Women.

Members will learn how to :

Discover their life purpose and choose the right major
Take care of mind, body, and spirit
Establish a work, school, life balance
Manage stress and finances
Navigate healthy relationships
Create a life and career plan for post college success
Be sexually healthy and empowered
Improve self-esteem
Become a powerful leader
Best use the many resources on campus
Handle common social struggles of college life with better balance
Become a phenomenal mentor and role model

Includes:
Monthly video lessons
Action plan to create and accomplish goals
Virtual Sister Circles
Access to exclusive offers, discounts and events
Peer to peer support systems and mentoring
Graduate with your P.H.D. in Phenomenal
Access to on going advice and support
Low time commitment (2hrs per month)

Visit www.phenomenally-u.com
Join Today!

Made in the USA
Middletown, DE
25 April 2021